The Terracotta Army

Critical Acclaim for *The Terracotta Army*

"In *The Terracotta Army* Gary Geddes's talent is to connect with some of those ancestral figures and give them to us...the poem cycle for the China figures is a NOBLE one...wonderful stuff... I was stunned and awed and this is so good."
—Margaret Laurence, novelist

"I was on the Commonwealth Poetry Prize Jury the year *The Terracotta Army* won the Americas Division Prize; it was the jury's unanimous choice, breathtaking in its imaginative reach, its verbal dexterity."
—W.H. New, critic and editor of *Canadian Literature*

"I have known Mr. Geddes for many years through his written work, especially his *Terracotta Army*, which I have found one of the most stunning works of poetry published in English-Canada in the last few years."
—Emile Martel, poet and Minister of Cultural Affairs, Paris

"Gary Geddes is unquestionably one of Canada's finest writers of epic and extended narrative poetry. *The Terracotta Army*...won the Americas Award for 1985 and is a brilliant example of his remarkable ability to maintain the tone, structure, and rhythms of the long, connected narrative. As a writer, anthologist, critic, teacher, and thinker, he is in a class with the best this country has to offer."
—Patrick Lane, poet

Also by Gary Geddes

Swimming Ginger, 2010
Falsework, 2007
Skaldance, 2004
Flying Blind, 1998
Active Trading: Selected Poems 1970-1995, 1996
The Perfect Cold Warrior, 1995
Girl by the Water, 1994
Light of Burning Towers, 1990
No Easy Exit, 1989
Hong Kong Poems, 1987
Changes of State, 1986
The Acid Test, 1980
War & other measures, 1976
Letter of the Master Horse, 1973
Snakeroot, 1973
Rivers Inlet, 1971
Poems, 1971

GARY GEDDES

The Terracotta Army

Copyright © 1984, 2010 by Gary Geddes.

All rights reserved. No part of this work may be reproduced or used in any form or by any means, electronic or mechanical, including photocopying, recording or any retrieval system, without the prior written permission of the publisher or a licence from the Canadian Copyright Licensing Agency (Access Copyright). To contact Access Copyright, visit www.accesscopyright.ca or call 1-800-893-5777.

These poems were first published by Oberon Press in 1984. Some of the poems in this collection first appeared in *Poetry Australia*. The entire sequence was dramatized and broadcast independently by both CBC and BBC radio.

Images are interpreted from photographs appearing in *Terra-Cotta Warriors & Horses at the Tomb of Qin Shi Huang*, first edition 1983, published by Cultural Relics Publishing House.
Calligraphy by Shuai Lizhi.
Cover and page design by Julie Scriver.
Printed in Canada on FSC certified paper containing recycled content.
10 9 8 7 6 5 4 3 2 1

Library and Archives Canada Cataloguing in Publication

Geddes, Gary, 1940-
The terracotta army / Gary Geddes. — 2nd ed.

Poems.
Originally publ.: Ottawa: Oberon Press, c1984.
ISBN 978-0-86492-634-0

I. Title.

Gary Geddes would like to thank the Ontario Arts Council for its assistance and also those, in Canada and the People's Republic of China, who made it possible for him to meet the underground soldiers and listen to their voices.

Goose Lane Editions acknowledges the financial support of the Canada Council for the Arts, the Government of Canada through the Book Publishing Industry Development Program (BPIDP), and the New Brunswick Department of Wellness, Culture, and Sport for its publishing activities.

Goose Lane Editions
Suite 330, 500 Beaverbrook Court
Fredericton, New Brunswick
CANADA E3B 5X4
www.gooselane.com

陶俑军队

Introduction

In the summer of 1981, with the help of Richard Liu, I organized the first formal tour of seven Canadian writers to China. My companions on this trip — accomplished poets, novelists, short story writers, and editors — were Alice Munro, Adele Wiseman, Patrick Lane, Robert Kroetsch, Suzanne Paradis, and Geoff Hancock. We had to go begging at home for funds to get there, but once in China we were treated as special guests by the Chinese Writers Association: fêted, housed, and chaperoned to literary gatherings, important landmarks, and the homes of famous writers.

Because the Bamboo Curtain was newly lifted, the phenomenon of international visitors was new to China, and foreign guests were closely watched. So it was a surprise to us, and to our hosts, not to have been relegated to the confines of *Beijing Youyi Binguan*, the old Soviet-style dormitory otherwise known as The Friendship Hotel. Seven unaccompanied *laowai* were still an unusual sight for most Chinese, especially when the foreigners showed up singing and dancing in a back alley in one of the *hutongs*.

Out for an unofficial evening stroll, our group steered towards the sound of music, where two young men perched on wooden crates were tentatively trying out some chords on a beat-up classical guitar. Assuming all Westerners knew how to play this instrument, they immediately handed the guitar to me. To protect the West's reputation, I was obliged to mask my ignorance and embarrassment by strumming a few chords and belting out the lyrics of "Red River Valley," unaware that this song had been recently translated and popularized by a Chinese singer. As Adele, Geoff, and the others came to my rescue, significantly increasing both the volume and quality of the performance, Patrick Lane, in jeans and a weathered straw hat, began to do a lively jig on the spot. Our performance, such as it was, brought a huge round of applause from several hundred curious locals, who materialized out of nowhere to investigate. I'm sure we could have continued into the night, but my repertoire was soon exhausted and, out of politeness, we gave the guitar and stage back to the two young men.

One of the principal stops on our literary excursion was the archaeological site outside Xi'an, the ancient capital of Chang'an in the Wei River Valley, where an underground army of approximately 8,000 terracotta soldiers and horses had been discovered quite by accident when farm workers were sinking a well.

A structure resembling an airplane hangar had been built to protect the pottery figures while they were carefully unearthed and reconstructed. It was deeply moving to see an arm or head emerging from the earth or a small cluster of terracotta body parts half cleared of two millennia of sediment. Some of the configurations resembled the horrifically beautiful sepia photos of trench warfare from World War I.

Columns of warriors, some of them already reconstructed and set in place, stood in rows, looking down the long corridor to eternity — to a moment when war would be no more, and when it would be viewed as one of the quaint aberrations of our primitive ancestors.

I could not speak. If I'd been able to say anything at all, never mind articulating the maelstrom of emotions that welled up in me, it would have been to utter a brief prayer requesting that the gifted companions flanking me be struck blind and dumb. Instead, I experienced both exhilaration at the spectacle and the depressing conviction that Patrick, Robert, or Suzanne were already giving imaginative shape to the terracotta warriors in their heads.

As it happened, my unuttered prayer was partially answered. None of the others who submitted work for *Chinada: Memoirs of the Gang of Seven*, the published account of our journey, had chosen to write about this unique encounter with history in Xi'an.

Shortly after *Chinada* appeared in print, I had some unexpected visitors in the reconverted chicken coop and horse barn where I did most of my writing. Each had an urgent message for me, not only about the first empire, but also about the potter who masterminded the placement and construction of Emperor Qin Shi Huang's posthumous insurance policy, the massive army that would protect him or, at least, scare off 'unfriendlies' in the afterlife*.

The potter's name, I learned, was Bi, though he was often referred to affectionately as Lao Bi, or Old Bi. From what these insistent but disembodied voices had to tell me, Lao Bi was a strange mixture of artist and anarchist, wit and iconoclast, as capable of understanding the psychology of his subjects as he was of capturing their appearance and essence in clay. Bi's iconoclasm — a peculiar term to apply to a sculptor, who is a maker rather than a breaker of images — lay in his determination to insist on the individual characteristics of the men he sculpted, in his resistance to the pressures to mass-produce an army of clones or look-alikes.

As the stories unfolded, they took the form of run-on rather than closed couplets (which would have been the Chinese method). I felt I needed the freedom of the more open form and that the soldiers deserved it too; besides, the couplets had an appropriately military aspect on the page. Since double-ninth day is special on the Chinese calendar, I thought nine couplets would suffice for each soldier to have his say, in what — because the Chinese, like Texans, do everything in a big way — I would come to call my Chinese sonnets. Within these confined forms, much would transpire: debates about the abuse of power and the meaning of art; the yin-yang dance of narrative and silence; the sanctity of the idiosyncratic self in the face of conformity; and, yes, a belief in the permanence of memory.

---

* In Pinyin, the romanized spelling of Chinese words, the 'Q' of the emperor's name and dynasty is a 'ch' sound, as in Ch'in; the 'X' as in Xi'an is a 'sh' sound.

The Terracotta Army

CHARIOTEER

So they call you layabouts a standing army;
there's more life in this terracotta nag

than in the whole first division. With that,
Bi leapt on the back of a cavalry pony he had fired

the previous day and dug his heels into the outline
of ribs. I wouldn't have been surprised

to see it leap into action and clear the doorway
with the potter shouting death to the enemy.

Most of the animals were cast from a single mould
and could be distinguished one from the other

only by the application of paint and dyes. I took
exception to this and remarked that, as charioteer,

I found more distinctive characteristics in horses
than in men. Bi swung his legs over the neck

and dropped to the ground. He was no taller
than the ponies he fashioned. Then, with a flourish,

he drew a green moustache on the horse's muzzle
and fell about the pottery amused by his own joke.

持矛武士

SPEARMAN

Before double-ninth day, my measure was taken
in a single sitting, so sure were Lao Bi's

eye and hand. The tenth month I returned
with armoured vest and spear and struck a pose

that pleased him so much he laughed out loud
and threw his wineskin at my feet.

He called me the youngest of the Immortals
and promised me a place in the glory-line.

The likeness was uncanny — not just the face,
but the way the sleeves bunched up at the wrists,

the studs and fluted leather of the shoulder pads.
I was drawn to it again and again, as if by magic.

One day, without warning, we left for the frontier
and I felt a greater reluctance

to part with his pottery replica of myself
than I had in taking leave of my village.

Bi used to slap me on the back and say,
you're too serious to be a soldier.

衛士

GUARDSMAN

At first I did not like him and put it down
to the arrogance of the creative mind,

his not mine. I'd been the previous day,
guarding the entrance to Qin Shi Huang's tomb,

where the artisans and craftsmen were at work
fashioning god knows what final luxuries

for the imperial afterlife. By the sounds of it,
they were feeling no pain. I mentioned this

quite casually, by way of small talk,
to the master potter as he examined my skull

and he exploded like a devil, threatening
to cut off my head for more detailed study.

Needless to say, I wasted no time absenting myself
from his presence and stopped in for a drink

at my quarters. They told me the tomb was finished
and the great door had been dropped into place,

sealing in every artist and workman employed there.
My hands flew, of their own accord, to cover my throat.

MINISTER OF WAR

I was a young man on the make, a brain for hire,
a travelling politician. I saw my chance,

adopted Qin, advised the death of the feudal tenure,
not to mention purges and the burning of books.

I scorned the golden mean of men like Mencius
and learned my politics from rats in the latrine;

yet I had respect enough for the written word to know
that old records and systems are better destroyed

than left to seed rebellion and discontent in the period
of transition. The same logic applied to scholars

and authors, those masters of anamnesis, or recall.
I kept the Emperor occupied with toy soldiers

and the arts, or fears of death and court intrigue,
while the real politics unfolded as I know it would:

highways, taxes, centralization, promotion by exam.
He might have stopped my war against the past,

but I saw to the depths of his and all men's hearts,
where artist lies down, at last, with bureaucrat.

LIEUTENANT

You might call me a jack-of-all-the-arts:
I paint, draw maps, sing, write a fair poem.

I skipped basic training because of the length
of my tongue and managed to nab a commission

right away in the reserve. I can toss off a lyric
or forge an epic in a single afternoon,

still observing the unities. Once I entered
the Emperor's competition and almost made it

to the finals. As far as visual arts are concerned,
I'm no slouch either. I've been known to sketch

enemy encampments in pitch black, still mounted,
give an accurate impression of slaughter

on the battlefield, avoiding dangerous skirmishes
and ignoring cries for help in order to complete

my precious record. The potter was not impressed.
Learn to write with this, he said, positioning

my hands on the jade hilt of an ornate sword,
the enemy has not yet learned to read.

PAYMASTER

We stood beside the trenches and looked at the rows
of figures there, bronze horses harnessed in gold

and silver, some of the charioteers in miniature
with robes and hairstyles denoting superior rank;

then the pottery horses with their snaffle bits
and bridles of stone beads. These had been fired

in one piece, except for the tail and forelock.
Most of the men could be seen to wear toques

over their topknots. Kang, of course had abandoned
such fashions and stood there with an eternal leer

and his pot-belly showing through armour, rivets
forever about to pop. A sensualist. I was astounded

as usual by the loving attention to detail and asked Bi
what thoughts this assembled spectacle called up in him.

Counterfeit currency, he said. A life's work
that will never be seen, poems tossed in bonfires.

A poem lives on in the ear, but a single push
will topple all of these.

INFANTRYMAN

We all marvelled at the courage of Jing Ke,
a serious man of letters who loved books

and often drank to excess with dog-butchers
and lute-players in the marketplace.

To please the Crown Prince Tan of Yen, who feared
the imminent demise of his kingdom by Qin,

Jing Ke agreed to undertake a daring plot
to assassinate the emperor. Delivering the head

of Qin's hated enemy General Fan in a box,
Jing Ke unrolled a map of the Yen territories

to be ceded. When the concealed dagger appeared
Jing Ke snatched it up and grabbed the sleeve

of the emperor, but the cloth tore in his hand
and his advantage was lost. Bi laughed

at this turn of events and made some remark
about the advantages of shoddy workmanship.

We tended to ignore his smart-ass comments
and asides, but the irony was not lost on us.

MESS SERGEANT

It was not so much the gossip that attracted me
to Bi's pottery, though there was plenty of that:

news of the latest atrocities against the people,
rights and property abolished, heads of children

staring vacantly from terraces, dismembered corpses
turning slowly in the current along the north bank

of the Wei. Rather it was a sort of clearing house,
a confessional, where our greatest fears were exorcised

piecemeal through the barter of objective detail.
I remember the day when word came of the taking

of Yen. Streets ran with the colour of Qin's revenge.
The lute-player, Gao Jianli, who had plucked Jing Ke

on his way to assassinate the emperor, was blinded
and forced to serenade the victors without ceasing,

blood still running down his face and arms.
Not a sound was heard in the pottery, except the crackle

of logs burning and the sizzle of spit as the last
moisture escaped from the baking clay figures.

MILITARY HISTORIAN

And so he standardized everything — axes, measures,
even the language itself. Six of this,

six of that, the uniform evils of power.
What can you say about a man who would burn

books, and the keepers of books? So great
was his fear of chaos and the unknown

he was a dupe for any kind of mumbo-jumbo
and excess. One of the wily magicians at court

convinced Qin he could find the fabled Island
of Immortals, but must take along the price

not only of gold and silver in great abundance,
but also a host of beautiful youths of both sexes.

Qin complied. Nothing more was heard of them.
The emperor put out that they were lost at sea,

but others amongst us presumed that the magician
had set himself up nicely on the islands of Fu Sang.

All this came to light much later, when Qin
died at the coast, vainly looking out to sea.

兵器 匠

BLACKSMITH

Bi remarked on the lethal aspect of the crossbow,
whose bronze trigger mechanism I'd just improved.

Tests had been done that morning on criminal types
who'd failed to comply with laws on standardization.

At short range the crossbow sent a heavy arrow
through the breasts of five men with surprisingly little

loss of speed; it was equally efficient on two others
in full armour, standing back to back outside the gates

of the Afang palace. I received a rousing cheer
from the assembled soldiers and nobility;

even the castratos pressed into service in the grounds
and gardens seemed more than slightly impressed.

Bi was sweating profusely and I thought he looked
rather pale in the dim light as he worked on details

of the armoured vest of a kneeling crossbowman.
Where is the dragon, rain-bringer, lord of waters

when we need him, the potter muttered to himself,
wiping the blade of the chisel on his leather apron.

HARNESS-MAKER

The plot to assassinate Qin Shi Huang
was a regular topic at the pottery.

Bi used it as an occasion to sound off about one
or other of his pet theories. What did I tell you,

he said one morning, unwrapping the four bridles
I had just delivered, a man who hangs out

with drunkards and ne'er-do-wells can't be all bad, eh?
No wonder his royal highness never sleeps in the same bed

two nights in a row. And his concubines —
what a waste! How can a man with so much on his mind

keep up his standard of performance? I have it
in strictest confidence from the younger sister

of his current favourite that, contrary to legend,
the Dragon of Qin is nothing but a worm.

Talk of this sort was confined to a trusted few,
including several peasants who made daily deliveries

of wood and bricks. One, brother of conscript Chen Sheng,
squatted like a coiled spring in the corner, grinning.

谋士

STRATEGIST

Avoid precipitous cliffs, marshes, quagmires, thickets;
at all times, make the terrain work to your advantage.

Arrive first and lie in wait, rested, fully alert.
Tempt the enemy into the open with shows of weakness.

Don't neglect spies, alliances, the impact of banners, gongs,
drums; detach a flying column, if needed, for a rout.

Better yet, win the war without fighting at all.
Information's the thing. What weapon or scaling-device

can replace the trained ear? Nothing, at least
not in my books. There is no sure defence against a good

pair of eyes. The five factors can remain constant,
and the Five-Year Plans, but what are the economies of war

when increased levies exhaust a people's substance
and spirit and bring the aggressor to his knees

before the enemy? Remember, prolonged war is folly;
so, too, is laying siege to a walled city.

Without these principles the whole empire, not just
the imperial army, will be in ruins.

密探

SPY

I'd read Sun Tzu,
that was my mistake,

read his *Art of War*
and committed it to memory.

Li Si was impressed; otherwise,
he might have left me alone

tending what few books remained
in the imperial library.

I was without status, no beauty either,
nondescript, down at the heels,

nobody's idea of a good time,
but I had my uses.

I was designated Category Five,
the surviving spy,

and ambled freely between the court
and Bi's establishment,

letting my body go to pot
but not my cover.

COMMANDO

My youngest brother disappeared without a trace
after the first recruitment. He was a musician

of no small promise, had anyone bothered to inquire,
and might have piped the hearts of simple men

to final victory or wrapped their deadly wounds in notes
of purest silk. Did he lend his flesh to the rubble

of a wall or make his bones instruments of war?
Don't ask. The new carts rattled by on their standard

axles, half-empty. Next they bred a line
of uniform slaves. Forced labour and conscription

destroyed the base of agriculture, brought revolt.
Who's to say it wasn't for the best?

You can tell by the lightness of my armour
I'm a crack trooper, trained to take the initiative

in battle. I prayed daily my strength would win
sufficient honours to bring me into the presence

of Qin and his bloody Councillor, to strike
a chord that's truly worthy of my brother.

徒手武士

UNARMED FOOTSOLDIER

Education does not win battles or put bread
on the table. I was a student once, I know.

I had my champions, my favourite causes;
the afternoons I was not gallivanting in full heat,

I spent debating the meaning of the universe.
Why did I bother? There's nothing quite like war

to clear the head — or remove it. I was drafted,
I became the perfect machine, a precision tool

for the mechanics of death. I was programmed
to kill. I did not need spear or crossbow:

a well placed blow would kill an ox or man
instantly; my special kick was called

the eunuch-maker. Still, my previous studies
were not entirely in vain. I was able to apply

the psychology I'd learned to outwitting the enemy
and, of course, my rivals within the ranks.

The potter read my story to the letter:
poised, unbalanced, deadly hollow.

CAPTAIN OF THE GUARD

Is there no aesthetic consistency any more,
that's what I want to know.

I registered a complaint, after the first sitting,
that he had taken more time braiding the tail

of a cavalry pony and stippling the sandals
of a kneeling warrior than he had taken

getting the fine detail of this face, which
has turned more than pottery heads in its time.

The next thing I know he's put the head
of that ugly recruit, now bearded, on the six-foot

frame of an officer and recorded for posterity
my untrimmed growth of whiskers.

No, I don't think it was the booze, at least
not primarily. A man like that creates

his own demons and opiates. Realist or formalist —
choose your poison. Was Qin drunk

when he shaved a mountain that thwarted him
and had it painted red, as a warning to all nature?

百夫长

UNIT COMMANDER

I was never too keen about the shape of my ears,
the way they hang there like two horseshoes

someone had stuck on as an afterthought,
so I can't say I was anxious to be duplicated

by this barbarous Southerner, whose words fell
about my feet like shards, kiln-dried and jagged.

We talked at length about Qin's appropriations,
not just the women, the art and the slaves

acquired from the defeated princes, but also designs
of palaces and gardens ordered to be copied

and reproduced in Xianyang, as if a man
could live in more than one house at a time.

He raged against the slipperiness of Immortals,
even immortal rats in their underground mazes;

then he went on, too long according to my notes,
about lack of imagination among peoples of the north,

how even into death they must carry a representation
of the living world. I couldn't believe my ears.

軍書

QUARTERMASTER

Seize reality in the act,
embrace its opposites like a lover,

without moderation. That's the ticket.
Though the flesh be captive,

insurgent thoughts invade the palace grounds,
storm the reviewing-stand. Freedom is born

in the anarchy of spilled blood.
Did I say that, or was it Master Bi?

He spoke so close to my ear as he applied
the clay to mould my features that his ideas

washed over my brain as if I were a puppet.
Certainly I don't remember propositions

of that sort troubling my professional self,
whose sole task was the dispensing of goods,

not words: weapons, food, clothing, rivets, lumber,
and sundry items for the conduct of war.

And no-one ever came to my tent and said:
Hey, buddy, give me a new idea, size five and a half.

ARCHER

He told me the Emperor's eunuch had paid a visit,
then Qin Shi Huang himself, disguised

as a standard bearer. I was half-mad with curiosity
to know what had transpired between them; instead,

I made some joke about the Great Qin
apprenticing to a potter. Bi mimed the action

of the crossbow and told me I was on target
as usual. Damn it, he shouted,

the man is hedging his imperial bets!
He knows he'll be judged by the company he keeps,

even underground. I told him I had neither the power
nor the inclination to fashion a god, simple as that.

Never mind, it's done. He's given me a month
to reconsider, while he swims and scans the seas

for some immortal vessel. Here Bi took my hand
in his terrible grip as if it had been an injured

bird. I felt his breath on my face as he spoke:
A man must know where his destiny lies, eh?

烽火臺斥候

LOOKOUT

For days he could not be found and was rumoured
to have returned to his boyhood home near Guilin,

where he had been a fisherman. Others claimed
he was sleeping off a drunk. Nothing was mentioned,

but his hand seemed less steady and his eyes
had a faraway look. Don't consider it odd if I dwell

overlong on your face, he said, it is perhaps my last
and will accompany me to the land of the White Snake.

He asked if I believed in astrology and practised
the lively arts. I told him I was a simple lookout

who could spot signs of movement a long way off
and keep a warning beacon alive in all kinds of weather

but, beyond that, I had no theories or opinions.
It occurred to me he might be a bit deranged,

what with working near all that heat and fumes.
Then he told me things about myself that scared me

and some that sent me back thinking I wasn't such a bad
chap, after all. You can't fault a man for that.

鼓手

REGIMENTAL DRUMMER

He refused, of course, to acknowledge the likeness
and huffed a good deal when I mentioned it.

I supposed he had a cousin in the imperial guard
but recalled a conversation weeks before

when he'd claimed to have no living relatives.
This is my family now, he'd added, pointing

to several terracotta figures in the corner.
But there wasn't the slightest doubt:

this unarmed soldier, turned slightly to reduce
the target area, legs apart, hands ready to parry

or strike a blow, was none other than Bi himself.
Portrait of the artist as master of martial arts,

in the front line, ready for anything, even his warts
rescued from oblivion. We drank a lot of wine

that night and danced around the pottery, reciting
poems, beating drums for the unknown soldier.

A slight smile played around the lips and I found myself
winking at the copy instead of the original.

GENERAL

If this is what we have evolved toward,
I have to laugh. The illusion of full knowledge

gave us a sinister edge; soon we became
the crassest of materialists and could tolerate

neither doubt nor disturbing hypothesis. In a word,
vulgar. How easily the innocent joy of the enthusiast

gives way to the intolerance of the true believer.
We began, like all the others, with a vision:

unification, call it what you will. The sorcery
of a fixed idea. For this we marched long years,

long miles, until, winning the war, we found we had
lost face. We became the new reactionaries,

eliminating, in short order, all the best minds.
Not all things are dangerous to the body politic;

being the son of a farmer, I should have remembered
that certain organisms must not only be allowed,

but also actively cultivated. Nature can be studied,
but never controlled or predicted with absolute precision.

MINISTER OF WAR 2

It's not because of superior rank or position
I'm allotted extra space to speak.

I merely have twice as much to answer for.
I was the right hand of God, responsible

for carrying out the wishes of the Leader.
I grew to be more than a soldier, or less —

a politician, which the potter describes cleverly
as a freak of nature that soars above the crowd

but still has ears close to the ground. Of course
I liked Master Bi. We were inextricably linked

by our humour and intelligence. He spoke in riddles
to confound the wise, but also to spread unrest

among the rank and file. I had plans, my own art
to pursue. I exercised decorum,

arranged for another artist to betray him.
Records were kept, tongues

loosed in the usual ways. The plot,
discovered, required a dénouement.

方士

CHAPLAIN

Someone will break us of the habit of war
by taking away our weapons

and we will march against the darkness
(or will it be light?) naked as newborn babes,

our tiny fists opening and closing on nothing.
The only certainty, even under the earth,

is change, whether it be cosmetic, paint
flaking away down the muted centuries

or something more violent that destroys the form
itself, icons of public and private selves.

With such thoughts I addressed the potter
on more than one occasion, thinking to shock him.

I'd given up the *Tao* and had even less time
for the ethics of Confucius in the new dispensation.

Rituals and ancestor worship are as useless to soldiers
as scapulimancy and tortoise-shell prophecy.

Only our vanity is monumental, the potter said,
and that, too, can be broken.

STANDARD BEARER

Who remembers names or issues now?
The wall that taxed us to the limits

stopped neither time nor barbarians.
Birds flew freely over the battlements,

testing the currents of non-aligned air;
so, too, did the arrows of our adversaries.

Then the enemy himself learned to fly —
by subtle propaganda into our hearts

or by invention into our very midst,
wreaking havoc like a berserker.

I joined the potter in his rest:
I broke his ranks but could not break his will.

Only our forms endure. And stubborn words
which hover and adhere, attend our passing

like faithful retainers. Remnants
of an age when the mind groped its way

in darkness, without maps of logic or conquest,
sweeping in its wake the relentless dust.